In the same series by Roland Fiddy:
The Fanatic's Guide to The Bed
The Fanatic's Guide to Cats
The Fanatic's Guide to Computers
The Fanatic's Guide to Dads
The Fanatic's Guide to Diets
The Fanatic's Guide to Dogs
The Fanatic's Guide to Golf
The Fanatic's Guide to Money
The Fanatic's Guide to Sex
The Fanatic's Guide to Skiing

Published simultaneously in 1992 by Exley Publications Ltd
in Great Britain, and Exley Giftbooks in the USA.

Reprinted 1992

ISBN 1-85015-273-X

Typeset by Brush Off Studios, St Albans, Herts AL3 4PH.
Printed in Spain by GRAFO, S.A. – Bilbao

Exley Publications Ltd, 16 Chalk Hill, Watford, Herts
WD1 4BN, United Kingdom.
Exley Giftbooks, 359 East Main Street, Suite 3D, Mount Kisco
NY 10549, USA.

Cartoons by Roland Fiddy
The Fanatic's Guide to
HUSBANDS

EXLEY

MT. KISCO, NEW YORK • WATFORD, UK

The Fanatic's Guide to Husbands

including Prospective Husbands, New Husbands, Used Husbands, Veteran Husbands, and Vintage Husbands.

Warning: Not recommended for Engaged Persons of a Nervous Disposition.

HUSBANDS COME IN ALL SHAPES AND SIZES

I'VE RUN OUT OF WHIMS FOR YOU TO ANTICIPATE, JAMES!

①

②

WELL, THANK GOODNESS *THAT'S* OVER!

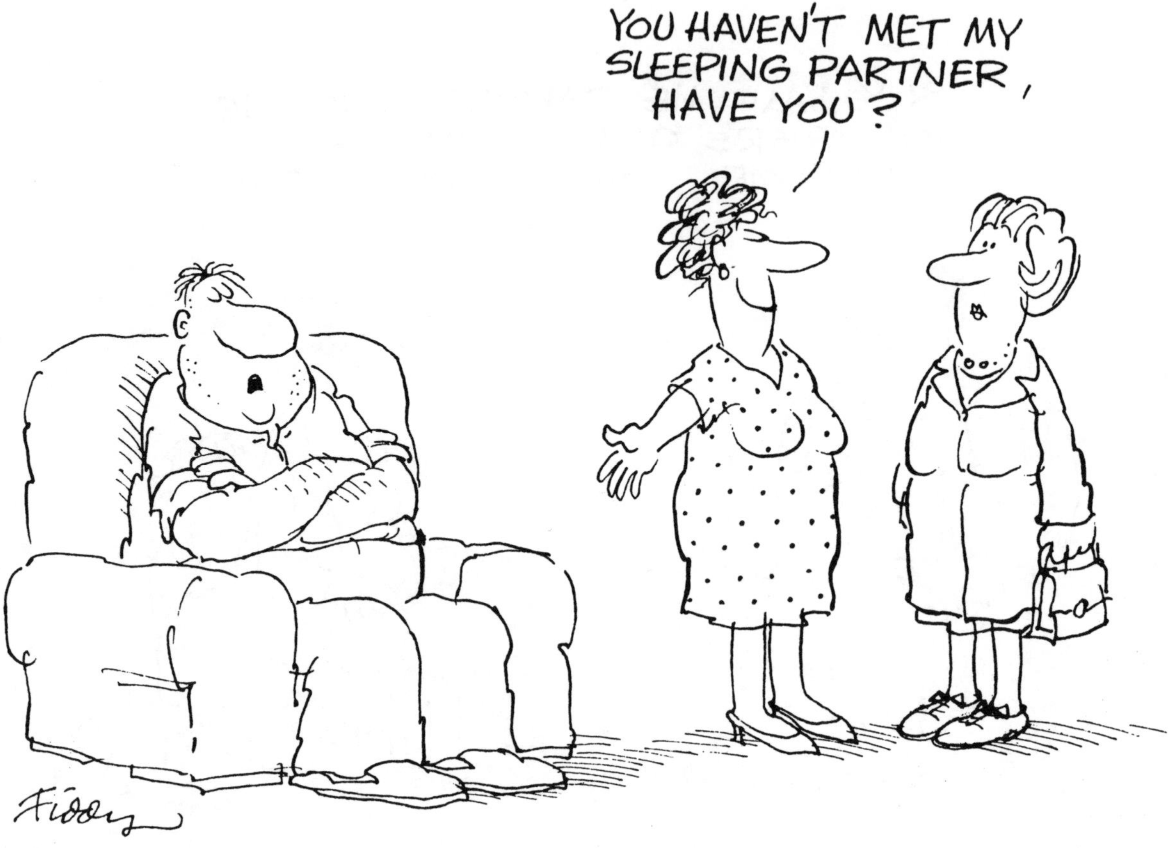
YOU HAVEN'T MET MY SLEEPING PARTNER, HAVE YOU?
Fiddy

1

2.

3.

4.

6.

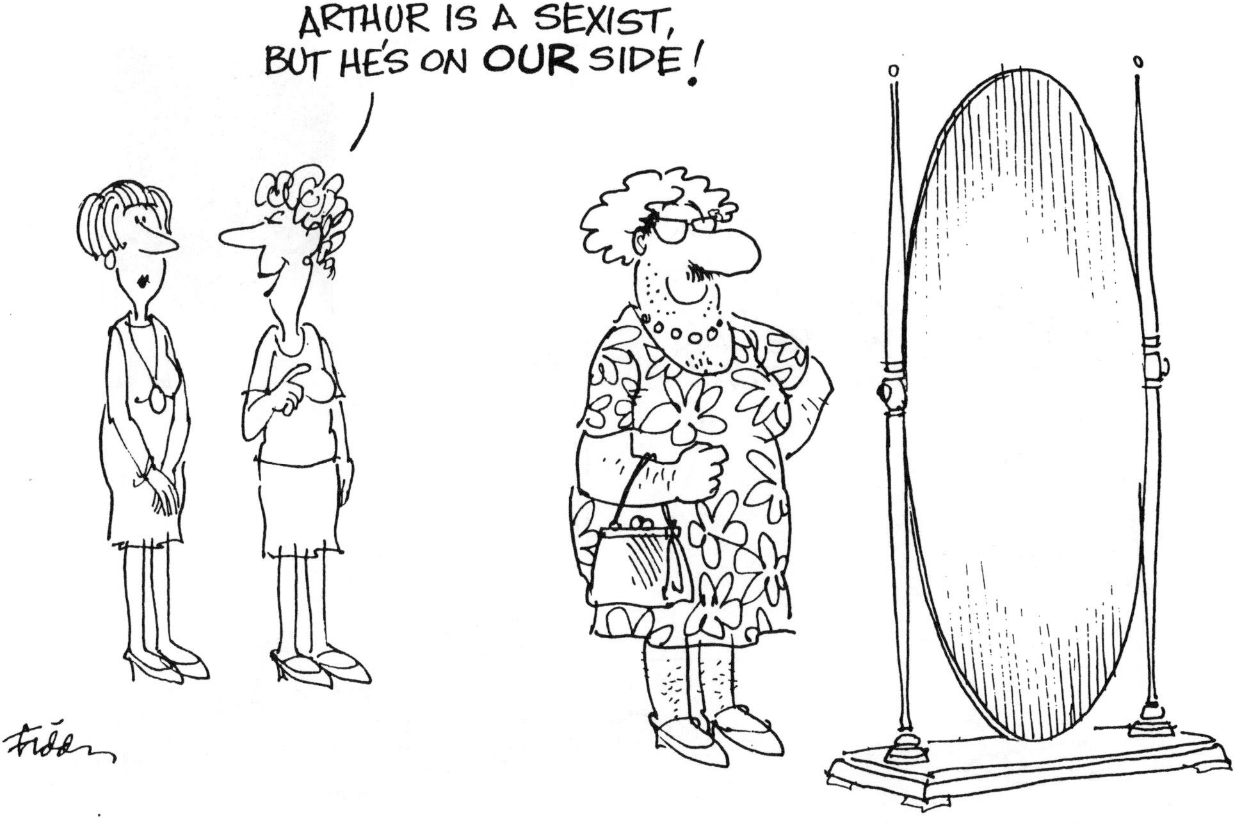
ARTHUR IS A SEXIST,
BUT HE'S ON OUR SIDE!

1. 2.

① ②

⑦

⑧

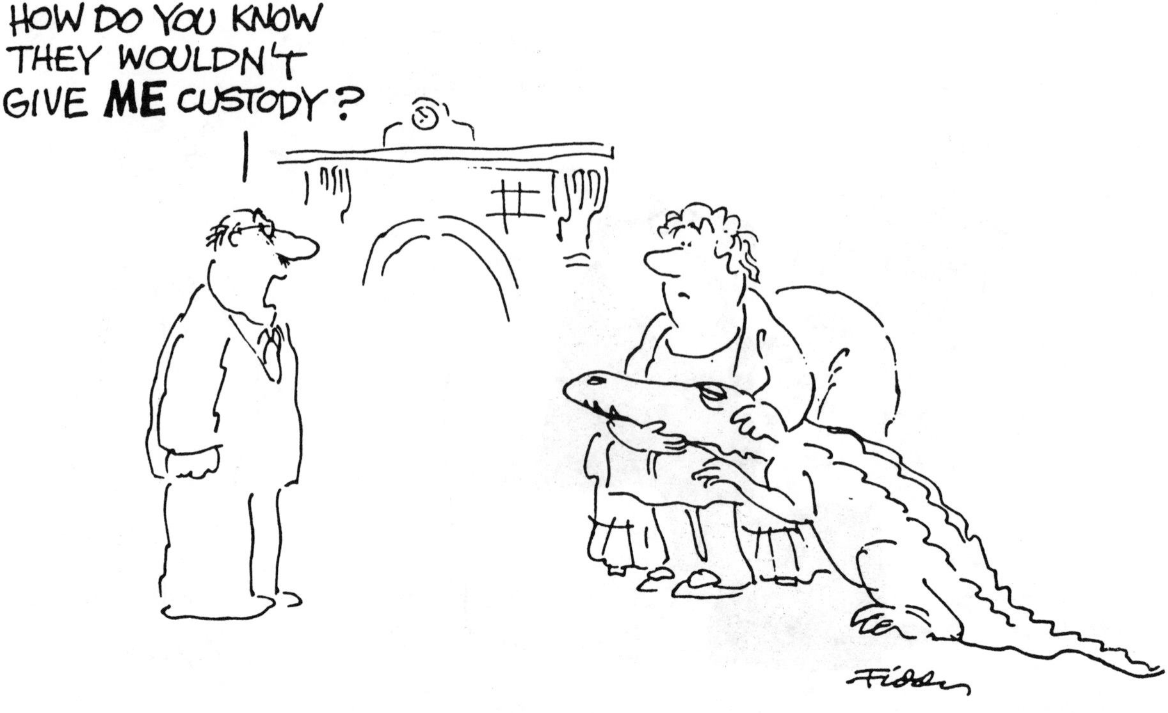
HOW DO YOU KNOW THEY WOULDN'T GIVE **ME** CUSTODY?
Fiddy

1.

2.

3.

4.

5.

6.

7.

SNAP!!

8.

Fiddy

Cartoons by Roland Fiddy

he Crazy World series
(4.99 £2.99 paperback)
here are now 13 different titles in this best
elling cartoon series - one of them must be
ght for a friend of yours...
The Crazy World of Cats (Bill Stott)
The Crazy World of Cricket (Bill Stott)
The Crazy World of Gardening (Bill Stott)
The Crazy World of Golf (Mike Scott)
The Crazy World of the Greens
   (Barry Knowles)
The Crazy World of the Handyman
   (Roland Fiddy)
The Crazy World of Hospitals (Bill Stott)
The Crazy World of Housework (Bill Stott)
The Crazy World of Marriage (Bill Stott)
The Crazy World of Rugby (Bill Stott)
The Crazy World of Sailing (Peter Rigby)
The Crazy World of Sex (David Pye)
The Crazy World of Skiing
   (Craig Peterson & Jerry Emerson)

Great Britain: Order these super books from your local bookseller or from Exley Publications Ltd, 16 Chalk Hill, Watford, Herts WD1 4BN. (Please send £1.25 to cover post and packing on 1 book £2.50 on 2 or more books.)

Roland Fiddy

Roland Fiddy is a freelance cartoonist and illustrator. He was born in Devon in Great Britain. His cartoons have been published in Britain, the United States, Germany, Holland and many other countries, and have received numerous awards at International Cartoon Festivals. At the Knokke-Heist Festival in Belgium in 1990 Roland Fiddy won First Prize, and, more recently, he was awarded the Prize for Excellence at Yomiuri Shimbun, Tokyo in 1991. His published books include all the *Fanatic's Guides* in the Exley series: *The Fanatic's Guide to The Bed, The Fanatic's Guide to Cats, The Fanatic's Guide to Computers, The Fanatic's Guide to Dads, The Fanatic's Guide to Diets, The Fanatic's Guide to Dogs, The Fanatic's Guide to Golf, The Fanatic's Guide to Husbands, The Fanatic's Guide to Money, The Fanatic's Guide to Sex* and *The Fanatic's Guide to Skiing*. He is also the cartoonist of *The Crazy World of the Handyman* and *The Crazy World of Love*, which are both published by Exley.